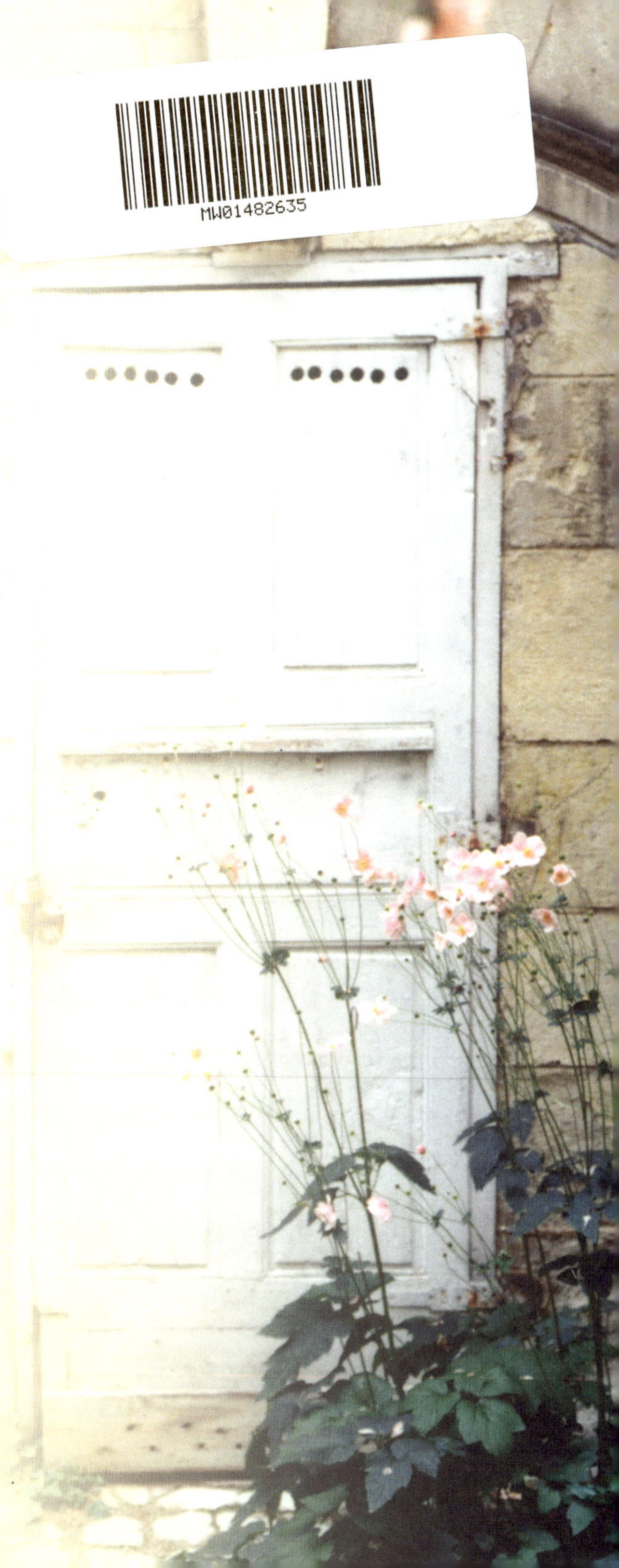

Shadow & Light

an illustrated journal

DREAMS are

journeys

that take one

far from

FAMILIAR

SHORES,

strengthening

the HEART,

empowering

the SOUL.

- unknown

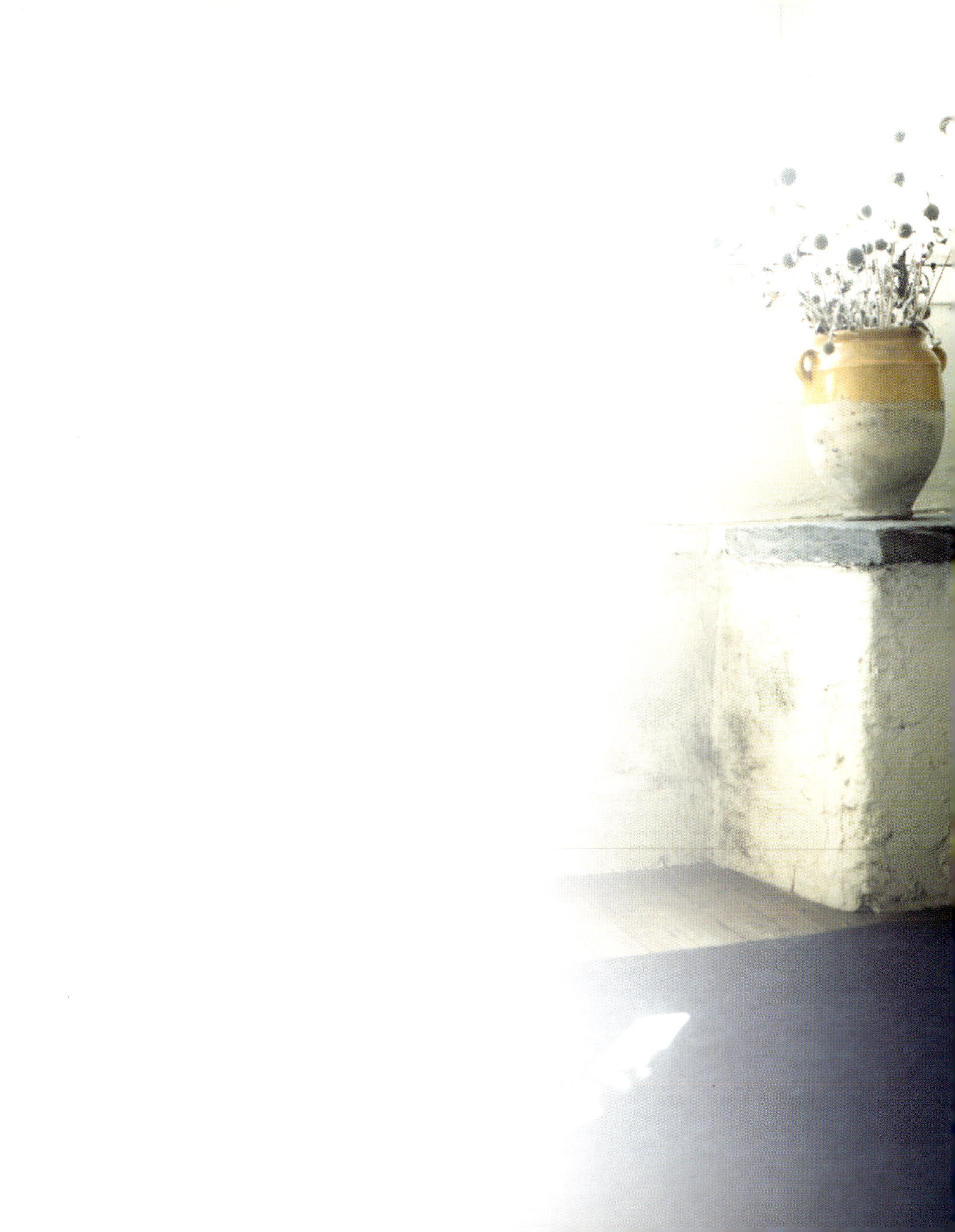

Quotes   Beware of Carl

BE HAPPY

for this MOMENT.

This moment

IS YOUR LIFE.

-Omar Khayyam

The GROWTH OF TRUE FRIENDSHIP may be a LIFELONG affair. —Sarah Orne Jewett

ANYONE

who says

SUNSHINE

brings

happiness

has never

DANCED

in the

RAIN.

— *Unknown*

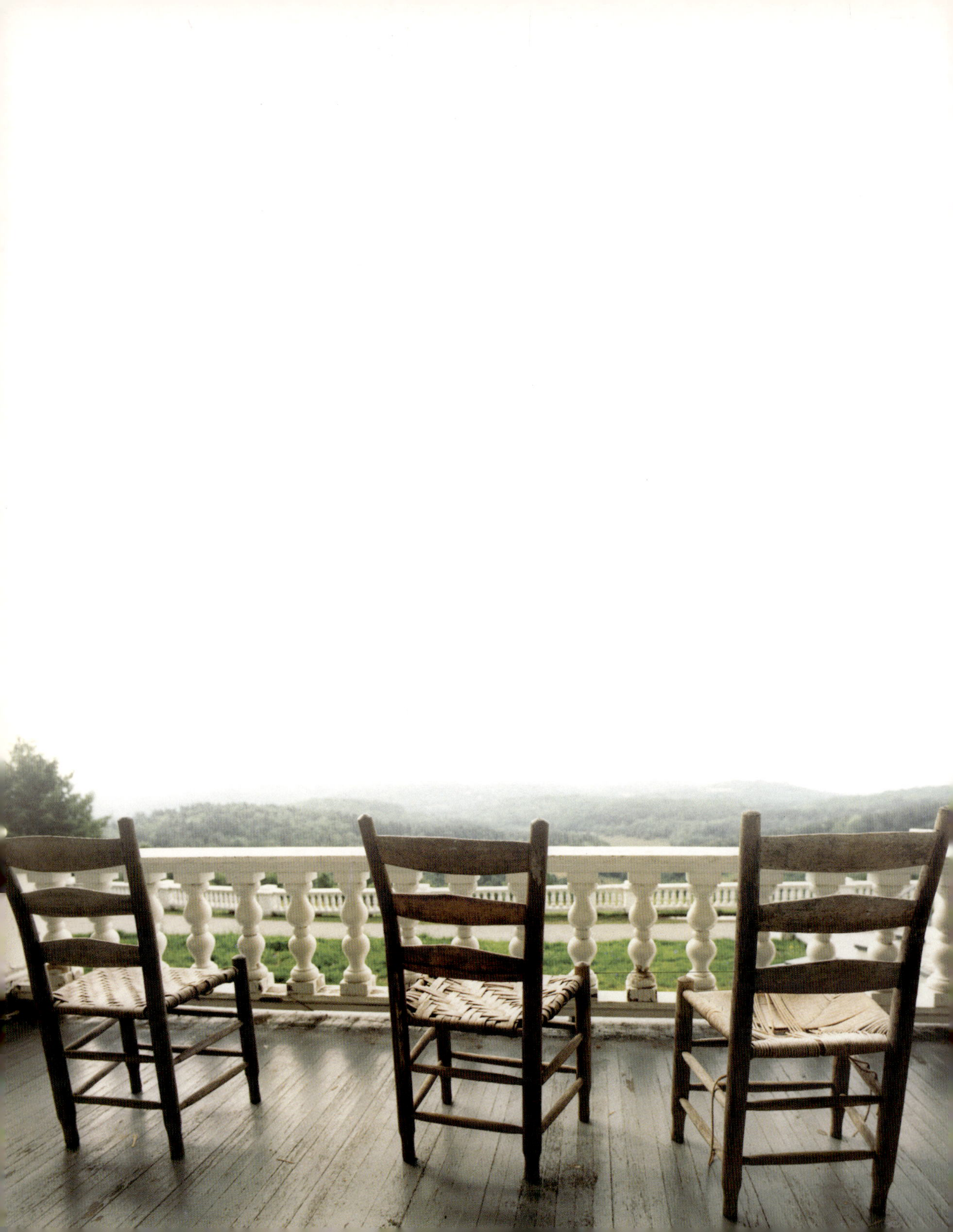

There are

THOUGHTS

which

are

PRAYERS.

There are

MOMENTS

when,

whatever

the posture

of the body,

the SOUL

is on

its knees.

- Victor Hugo

Stretch out your HAND and take the world's

vide GIFT of joy and BEAUTY. —Corinne Roosevelt Robinson

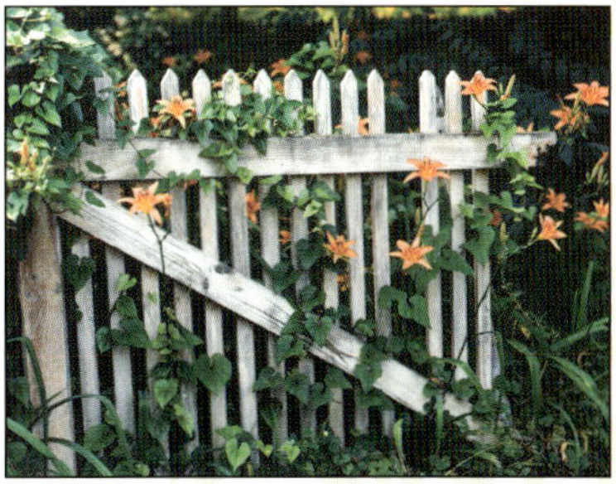

Go
confidently
in the
DIRECTION
of your
DREAMS.
Live
the LIFE
you have
IMAGINED.

-*Henry David Thoreau*

THINKING is the work of intellect, DREAMING is pleasure.   -Victor Hugo

Don't save anything for a special occasion,

being alive is the special occasion.

-unknown

LIGHT

always

FOLLOWS

darkness.

–Anonymous

WE TRAVEL

the world

in search

of what

WE NEED

and return

home

TO FIND IT.

–George Moore

The

FIRST

thing,

The

LAST

thing.

START

from

where

YOU

are.

-Dale Pendell

When you ARISE in the morning, THINK of what a privilege

it is to be alive: to BREATHE, to think, to enjoy, to LOVE.   —*Marcus Aurelius*

There are
two ways of
spreading LIGHT:
to be
the CANDLE
or the MIRROR
that reflects it.

-*Edith Wharton*

May your life be CROWDED with unexpected JOYS.   *-H. Jackson Brown, Jr.*

FINISH

each day

and be done

with it.

You have

done what

you could.

TOMORROW

is a

new day.

You shall

BEGIN it

serenely

and with

too high

a SPIRIT

to be

encumbered

with

your old

nonsense.

—Ralph Waldo Emerson

Nothing

is worth

more

than

this

day.

-*Goethe*

Once
you have
tasted
flight,
you will
forever walk
the earth
with your
eyes turned
skyward,
for there
you have been,
and there
you will
always
long
to return.

-Leonardo da Vinci

The real voyage of DISCOVERY consists not in SEEKING new landscapes

but in having new EYES.

- Marcel Proust

DISCOVERY consists of looking at the SAME THING as everyone else and thinking something DIFFERENT.

–Albert von Szent-Györgyi

Make

EACH

DAY

your

masterpiece.

- John Wooden

THERE

is no

way to

happiness.

HAPPINESS

is the

way.

-Buddha

We

MUST

always

have

old

MEMORIES

and

young

HOPES.

- Houssaye

The JOURNEY is the REWARD.   *– Taoist saying*

You GAIN

strength,

courage,

and confidence

by every

EXPERIENCE

in which

you really

stop to

look fear

in the

face . . .

DO the

thing

you think

you

cannot

do.

-Eleanor Roosevelt

To finish
the MOMENT,
to find
the JOURNEY'S END
in every step
of the road,
to LIVE
the greatest
number
of GOOD HOURS,
is wisdom.

-Henry David Thoreau

FIND the seed
at the bottom
of your HEART
and bring
forth
a FLOWER.

-Shigenori Kameoka

PEACE.

It does

not mean

to be in a PLACE

where there

is no NOISE,

trouble

or hard WORK.

it means

to be

in the midst

of those things

and still

be CALM

in your HEART.

–unknown

ONLY

the feet

of the

VOYAGER

know

the PATH.

- East African Saying

LIVE in the present. LAUNCH yourself on every wave, find ETERNITY in each moment....

-Henry David Thoreau

Deborah DeWit Marchant's
artistic search began with photography
and journal writing. Her photographs
capture everyday scenes transformed
by the light that fascinates her.
Inspired by her daily life and
her travels, she has concentrated
on a signature range of subjects
that speak of our human need
for comfort, knowledge and freedom,
qualities that often do not co-exist.

All artwork by Deborah DeWit Marchant
Book design by Liz Kalloch